Glitter and
DARKNESS

Also by A.M. Forney

A.M. FORNEY

Forgiving
MADNESS

POETRY & PROSE

Glitter and DARKNESS

POETRY and PROSE
by A.M. FORNEY

300 SOUTH MEDIA GROUP

□ □ □

NEW YORK

GLITTER and DARKNESS

ISBN-13: 978-1-957596-26-6 (paperback)

Published by 300 South Media Group

To my family and those closest to me.
I love you all.
Too much peacocks.

TRIGGER WARNING

While my first book, Forgiving Madness, *contained dark themes,* Glitter & Darkness *delves into even more challenging and deeply personal topics. Some pieces are free from triggers, but others address sensitive subjects that may be difficult for readers. Your mental health is important – please proceed with care.*

Themes and Potential Triggers:
Sexual Assault
Narcissistic Abuse
Childhood Trauma
Mental Health Struggles
Death and Dying
Pet Loss
Infidelity
Alcohol Abuse
Miscarriage

I encourage you to prioritize your well-being and take breaks or skip pieces as needed.

TABLE OF CONTENTS

GLITTER & DARKNESS
the glitter in this project
is solely because of my kids
their love makes me write happy
before, I never did

TOO MUCH PEACOCKS

FAMILY TREE

Roman
my first born
first maternal bond
Avana
my first daughter
bright blue eyes and blonde
Titan
my baby and soulmate
made with a magical wand
Jack or Scarlet
my angel baby
watching from above
these four babies are
who I deeply love
my children are my lifeline
their love keeps me whole
it keeps me feeling warm inside
no matter how many times I'm told
I love you mommy
it always melts my heart
pulls at the strings
these four babies
are what true love brings

to the table
for all to see
I wear it across my chest
like a badge of honor
because it is
you are
you're my badges of honor
my pride and joy
Roman
Avana
Titan
Scarlet or Jack
everything to me
I cannot wait to continue
to watch you grow
into all you can be
and knowing that our angel baby
is above
sends us a deep feeling
of continuous love
watching their family
even though they couldn't be
doesn't mean
they're not forever on our family tree

MISSING OUT

I wish you could stay little
but I also want you to grow and see
how much I have sacrificed
to prove what you mean to me
I miss out on routines
laughs and funny times
sometimes, I don't know until you tell me
you've learned a new nursery rhyme
I'm sad and I hate that I have to miss out on such
things
I don't want to keep missing
I want to see what the future brings
Please don't hate me when you're older
because I wasn't always there
always know that the pain of absence
was extremely hard to bear

FOREVER BLESSED

thankful is an understatement
blessed isn't a strong enough word
to say I had a life before you
is totally absurd

·•·⋛·o⟩.ͅ.⟨o·⋚·•·

A FOURTH TIME

you'll be here soon
then, we can love on you
boy, has this been a journey
that we have gone through
you're worth every second
wouldn't trade anything at all
we've fallen three times
a fourth time, we will fall

ROMAN BLADE

you look at me and say mama
my heart, it simply melts
for that tiny, little word
makes me feel the best I've ever felt
you made me that word
gave me the highest title in life
right after your daddy gave me
my original first title, as wife
you're only two but you seem sixteen
you make me understand life
and what it all means
with a magic power, I'd slow down time
to keep you my baby
to keep you just mine
I love you, Roman Blade
trust, know and believe
those words will never fade
And my love will never leave

AVANA BROOKE

your eyes, crystal blue
shining up at me
you're the most perfect little girl
there ever could be
you run to me after work
to give me a hug
how could someone be born
such a gentle, love bug
I admire your beauty
I adore your soul
you, little girl
make my heart so very full

TITAN BLAZE

for the rest of my life
till the end of my days
I'll repeat I love you
always, Titan Blaze

MY SON

when I look into my son's eyes
it's a magical feeling
who was I without him?
where was he
while waiting for me to be his mother
did he choose me?
I've never been so lucky

RAINBOW BABY

we finally got a green light
to tell everyone about you
we were hesitant and nervous
because of what we had been through
you're not only our third
you're our technical number four
even though you're so small
we couldn't love you any more
you're our rainbow
our fifth heart
the reason it beats
you're proof that true love and strength
always defeats

FOR MY FAMILY

For my family
I will do whatever it takes
For them, I will
Heighten all of the stakes
They are the reason
For everything that I do
Without them
I'd be lost, without a clue
So when I say i'll do anything
Everything
It is to my word
That I stick
And I cling

FORGIVE ME, MY CHILDREN

I wasn't always patient
or fun to deal with
but forgive me
that was just a mother
trying her hardest
to love her children
to the best of her ability
keeping you safe
is my number one priority
if that makes you uncomfortable
forgive me
I need you with me
I need you to be okay
if that makes me the bad guy
forgive me

TOO MUCH PEACOCKS

you know that I love you
I know you love me too
but we needed a phrase to express
the depth at which we felt
this love
too much peacocks
is what we say
without saying it to each other
we cannot start our day
it's the last thing before bed
when we snuggle
and our prayers are said
too much peacocks
further than the galaxy
and longer that the time on a clock
Momma loves you forever
forever
too much peacocks

SWEET, ANGEL BABY

I lost you
I couldn't keep you here
I lost you
this fact brings me to tears
I lost you
was it something I did wrong?
I lost you
but I'll love you all along
along this journey
called life
for any wrong I felt I've done
you made me feel right
I'll forever be your momma
I love you
my sweet, angel baby

OCEANS AND MOUNTAINS

my heart, it flutters
when I watch you sleep
across oceans and mountains
for you, I would leap
always stay with me
slow down as you grow
my love for you is stronger
than you'll ever know

· • · ⋛· o)).ȯ.((o ·⋚· • ·

YOUR BIRTH

I've never known joy
like the day of your birth
for now, I know my purpose
being here, on this earth

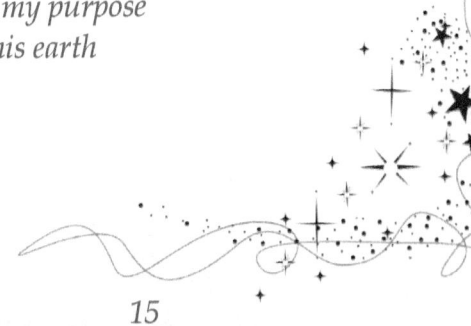

ALL I EVER WANTED

maybe I lost my temper
I may have even yelled
I just really wanted to know
that you, I had not failed
my worries and fears
I had hoped you didn't see
All I ever wanted
Is for you to look up to me

SOULMATE

you are my soulmate
I know that you are
I can see the past
and we go back so very far

JOY

You bring me light
You bring me joy
You is my little girl
And two little boys

TEARS OF JOY

I never cry
I never do
but I did cry
the moment I saw you
it was happy tears
I was full of joy
the instant I saw
my first little boy

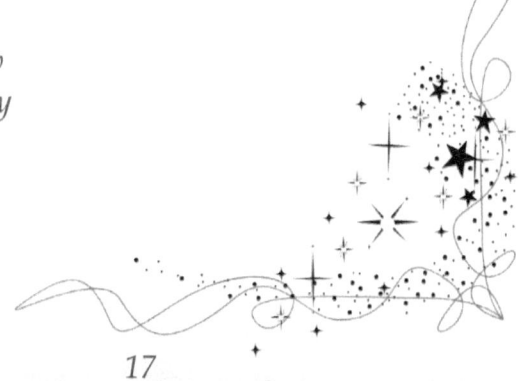

THE JOY OF A CHILD

The joy of a child
It comes, unmatched
Keep them close to you
When they grow, they won't be so attached
Or maybe they will, you never know
But keep them close
Close as they grow

.•. · ʒ· o)· ȯ. (o. ʒ. •·

MY KIDS

I love my kids
they know I do
and they love me
I know this too

MOTHER

mother
it's life's greatest title
to be the one who
takes care
loves
supports
the tiny souls
that they've created
the lives that they grew
so, be gentle with yourself, momma
they're them because of you

TO MY HUSBAND

NOVEMBER 2009

Back in November of 2009
A boy got the nerve to ask, "will you be mine?"
Fast forward through all the years that have passed
We never knew we'd be the first, only and last
To carry the vow
And rewrite the script
Still stronger than ever
When everything flipped
It'll only be a matter of time
Soon enough, they'll all see
There's no me without you
And no you without me
Overcoming it all and then, some more
Our love will conquer any obstacle that may be in store

10/16/15

On October sixteenth
They made a vow
And looking back
They're proud of how
Far they've come
How much they've grown
Back on that day
They couldn't have known
They'd go through the best
And go through the worst
But through it all
They had to put their love first

HUSBAND

I never wanted to get married
I never saw it for myself
But then
I met somebody
Who made me question
Life and my goals
I had none except to survive
Until after that point of meeting
When I was with him
I felt alive
I knew he was the one
And from that moment on
It was our life, we had begun
A house
Some dogs, cats
And kids
Wondering why from this
I hid
So long
Saying I didn't want any of it
When clearly, I did
It is like it was my calling
What I was meant to do

But husband
None of what I've accomplished
Is without you

STEP UP

When you realize that you've made someone feel
Lonely and depressed
The feeling is unreal
You don't want to be
The reason for that
So you put your own hurt aside
And step up to bat

COLD WIFE

He has a cold wife
She has a cold heart
She doesn't really get upset
When they have time apart
But that has nothing to do with him
It's because of her past
She knows she can be confident
Because she knows they'll last
So, with her cold heart
And with her frozen soul
She feels she needs to tell him
What he hasn't been told
She loves him and he is
Her other half
Even with all the jokes he makes
When she refuses to laugh
She remembers the good times
And the ones ahead
She loves that they go to sleep
In a full, loving bed
3 cats
3 kids
And them

The way it's meant to be
Our moment of impact
Was when you first asked her to be
Your wife
To marry you
She knew even back then
It was the best thing she'd do
She's sorry that she's a cold wife
But there is nobody else
She'd rather have in her life

I'M SORRY

I'm sorry for any wrongdoing I've done
I'm sorry for saying you weren't the one
I never thought I'd get to that place
Now, looking back
there's so much I'd erase
all I can do now is apologize
and hope that one day
you realize
that I'm sorry for all that I have done
and you are truly the only one
for which I want to spend my life
and that I am proud
to be your wife

RINGS

my rings are a reminder that he loves me to death
for him, I would give my last, single breath
our babies are what truly make my heartbeat
there is no war or battle that us five cannot defeat

.•.⟨.o⟩.ȯ.⟨o.⟩.•.

ULTIMATE GOAL

I woke up with a heart so big and so full
my family
as one
was the ultimate goal
a second chance
to get it right
explode with happiness
I think, I might

PRAYING

I've never felt so alone in my life
I was the best mother
I was the best wife
a stupid mistake set me back for how long
why the hell did I do it?
knowing it was wrong
I'm praying for answers and praying for strength
to repair my family, I'll go to any length
I want to wake up beside him, in bed with our kids
erase all the things that he never did
I need my family
and I need hope too
but when you're not getting answers
what else can you do?

FOR THE BIRDS

everything hurts and I'm really depressed
in all of my years, I've never been this stressed
can time just hurry up and pick up the pace?
heartbreaking to me that I can't see his face
I miss him so much that it hurts inside
on that dumb, drunken night, a part of me died
they say have faith, speak positive words
I'm almost to the point of saying, that shit is for the
birds
but I won't give up
I won't quit now
because in 2015, I made a vow
for better, for worse
through the thick and the thin
I have to be patient
and our love will win

NEAR AND DEAR

MY MOMMA

my momma's name is Brenda Lee
she has always been there for me
she's the one who taught me
most of what I know
to her, I am indebted
for helping me to grow
and all that she gave
I owe it to her
because of her, I was raised
to be strong and resilient
to weather the storm
to be the woman I became
after the day I was born

WADE

I have this uncle
his name is Wade
my bond with him
will never fade
he's been there for me
in my times of need
there is not a bone in his body
that is riddled with greed
he has what I swear is the purest heart
fixing things, mostly cars
is his talent, it's his art
everyone should have an uncle Wade
the debt in my life
has always been paid
by his acceptance, his love and support
to express my reciprocation
this poem, is where I resort

FRAMILY

we tell our kids
they're an uncle or aunt
because going through life
we just know that we can't
leave them out of the journey
the good and the bad
the memories with them
are some of the best we've ever had
when friends become family
it's a newly found word
your life without them
the thought, totally absurd
so when the word is brought up
and you think it's silly
know that we don't
because they're framily

203

there's a place that raised me
where I learned who I was
who I wanted to be
that place holds the number
of 203
I'll never forget where I came from
but this place is where I formed who I am
I'll remember the memories
as long as I can

SPEAK OF THE ANGEL

Have you ever met someone
And instantly knew
That you'd get along
And it would stick like glue
They're an angel in disguise
And you love them more
Than they'll ever realize

519

so many traumas happened
at 519
so many things were saw that shouldn't be seen
it feels as if the house stole our innocence
stole who we were becoming
altered our fingerprints
but props to my mother
she was always loving
us no matter what
despite how we acted
she loves us
that fact is
truer than true
no matter what happened at 519

YOUR MEMORY

the drive-in movies
tea parties
and love
are memories I'm left with
know that you're up above
you're looking down
you're watching us
don't think your memory
was lost

WHEN THE SMOKE CLEARS

There may have been fights
There may have been tears
But I'm who will be standing
Up for you
When the smoke clears

LITTLE LIBRARY

there's a place you can go
and take a book
you can replace it
the one that you took
or you can simply take
and enjoy
that's what it's for
there's a certain joy
in borrowing from others
even if you return it
you don't have to replace
just pay it forward

BABY SNUGGLES

there is a feeling on earth
that you can get
from the snuggles
of littles if you will let
them crawl up on your lap
or lay on your chest
baby snuggles
are the feeling
that I love the best

UNFORGETTABLE

you are unforgettable
nothing about you is regrettable
you filled our hearts with pure love
and joy
you were our first fur baby
our favorite to play and enjoy

1804

this little house
became our home
but it is this house
that we've outgrown
when the day comes
to say goodbye
I'd be lying to you
if I said I won't cry
so much has happened
while being under this roof
I'll mourn all of that when we leave
and that is the truth
but I have to remember
have to keep alive
the memories that we made
while love was filling the inside
of the walls, the rooms, behind each door
the next house has a lot to live up to
but we know we need more
more space to live
more room to grow
but of 1804, I'll never let go

CLEARWATER

there's a beautiful place
that we used to go as kids
in the backseat
where my sister and I would sit
jamming to Shania
and other good tunes
remembering these trips
before they're gone too soon
lost in the memories
the time we had left
it all went so quick
I won't let myself forget

TRIPS

we used to go on trips
and we truly loved it
we had so much fun
and nothing was above it
but after the loss
the trips seemed to lessen
but on those vacations
we learned a lesson
that family is what matters most
and family
is who you should always keep close
because they can be gone
and you don't see it coming
even with warning
there is no halt to your loving
your memories
the good times
the trips were so fun
but her trip was taken up
in heaven, with the sun

GRANDMA

tea parties
trip to the beach
happiness seemed
so within reach

·•·≶·o)·ọ·(o·≷·•·

PAP PAP

he's blue
she didn't know the cause
not breathing
she had no idea, the loss

SHAKEABLE NOT BREAKABLE

We've been through so much
On this journey called life
We have experienced happiness
We have experienced strife
There have been falling outs
And bad words said
But back to each other is where
We are ultimately led
While our foundation may shake
It will never crack
And at least for me
I'll always have your back

POSITIVE WOMEN

Audrey
And Darby
are the positive women
who surround me
they lift me up
they are my rocks
their souls are
where my soul flocks
because it can sense that
they have good hearts
I hope we are friends forever
and that we never part

NEW JERSEY

there's a place where she goes
and she feels more alive
she can lie by the water
or take a little dive
into the sunshine
into the sand
with her family, she walks
they're all hand in hand
the boardwalk is peaceful
the beach, just as nice
to go there another year
never have to ask her twice

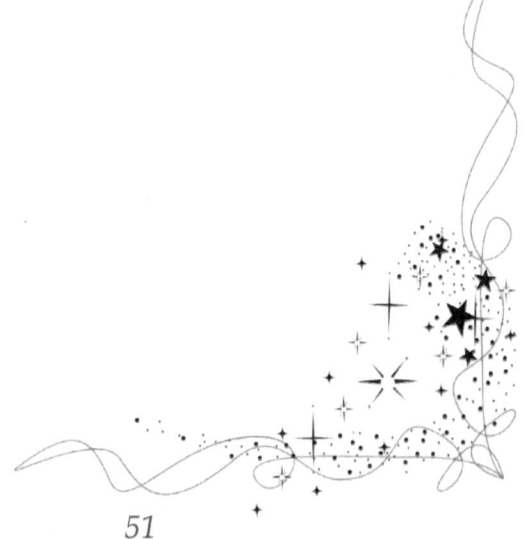

DEAR BRYCE

today, we said goodbye
but it isn't the end
you'll always be
our forever friend
to say you were the best
is putting it lightly
you may have crossed the bridge
but I think that you might be
happy and healthy
playing with all kinds of toys
please continue to watch over
Avana and the boys
we love you, Bryce
so very much
there isn't a single heart you met
that you didn't touch

OX

My husband surprised me
With the gift of a puppy
But now that we have him
I feel very lucky
He's a gentle giant
A miniature horse
When asked if I love him
I respond, "of course"
He's our protector
Our built in alarm
To this entire family
He'd never do any harm
He's a Saint Bernard
Of that, he is pure
We feel more protected now
Than we ever did before

CAT AND MOUSE

it seems it's a game
of cat and mouse
memories of you
all throughout the house
we love you
and we always will
the moment we lost you
time seemed to stand still
the game that this is
just doesn't seem real
it doesn't seem like
I'm allowed to feel
the hurt of losing
and also, the pain
but heaven was lucky
because an angel, they gained

WITHOUT LIMITS

a dog, a k9, a friend
no matter what you call them
they're there till the end
they love you without limits
whether it's long, cozy snugs
or a pet for a minute
they love you for what they can
feel from inside
your heart from a dog
you should never hide
they give the love back
you know it's true
you love your dog
they love you too

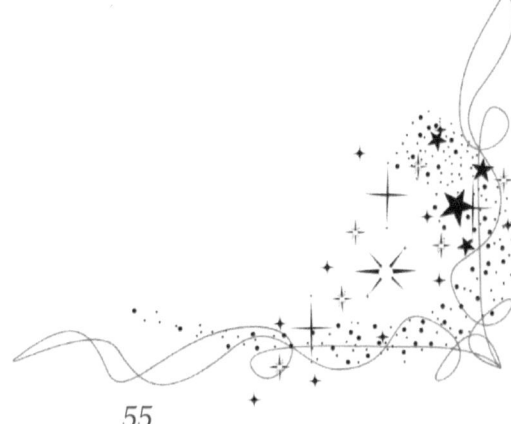

LONG DISTANCE FRIEND

I never thought it could be true
that you could grow close
to someone you never knew
before you made an Instagram account
but they're a long-distance friend
and their friendship amounts
to more than they could ever know
whether you ever meet or not
your friendship will continue to grow

UNCLE

my kids have an uncle
and I have a brother
who loves us and we love him
like no other
he used to stay with us
always around
but it's been silent for a while
nothing but the sound
of snapchat and text
message alerts
I'd like to say
and insert
that we miss you
we truly do
we miss you
and love you too
too much peacocks
is what we say
despite the distance
that will never change

YOU SHOULD RUN

it's starting again
the feeling that my skin
is ripping to shreds
what's coming from inside
the darkness that consumes my soul
that is my being
and you should run

INTENTIONALLY BLANK

WHAT YOU DO

keep what isn't yours
that is what you do
take from others until
they struggle to get through

·•·⸜·o⟩·ȯ·⟨o·⸝·•·

TOOK

I gave you all I could
you took, happily
it was all I had
yet, I made sure to give
now, with a guilty conscience
I hope you live

I THOUGHT

I thought the day that I heard
you didn't care anymore
that we weren't important
that you didn't love me
that you denied us
I thought it would hurt
thought it would tear at my soul
but all it did was free me
away from the chaos
away from the stress
my soul and heart are separate
but they want the same thing
they want goodbye

WHERE DO YOU GO?

where do you go
so late at night
wishing you weren't
but we know we are right
we know where you're going
we know what you're doing
no care of the kids
that you will ruin
do you think of us at all
when you're playing your games
being unfaithful
forgetting you gave your name
to our mother
the other half of your life
a stab to her heart
with your cold, cold knife

GOLDEN CHILD

From golden child
To the bottom of the pit
All you do is make me feel
Like literal shit
Like my existence is nothing
Like it doesn't matter to you
No matter if it's good or bad
That I go through
But you know what?
It doesn't matter anymore
I'll get over it
As I have before

DECAY

You aren't the dearest
I'll be the sincerest
when I tell you it is your fault
you caused this dismay
you caused this decay
of a family who mattered more

FIND HIM

follow him
find him
he's right there ahead
retrace his
steps
pay attention to where you're led

HATERS

BULLY

you pushed me out
right out the door
you made me think
I couldn't be more
I was all that I was able to be
but you pushed and pushed
you bullied me
I would have succeeded
I would have excelled
but you kept tormenting me
like I was living in hell
fast forward to now
I'm the best I can be
it's a wonderful feeling
that you have no hold over me

SPARKLE

The only people who try to dull your sparkle
Are the ones who live in darkness themselves

·•·≷·o)·ȯ·℄o·≷·•·

UNSTOPPABLE

How do you know you're unstoppable?
When they try to hold you back

·•·≷·o)·ȯ·℄o·≷·•·

WEIRD

People who get mad at your happiness are weird

STEPPING STONE

you used her as a stepping stone
and that's okay
you avoid her, ignore her
then pretend close, you'll stay
like you're close
still friends
like you didn't burn the candle at both ends
she was all you had
when you had no one else
you should try to remember
because you will end up by yourself
she won't be there
she'll be a memory
upon a dusty shelf

WHAT ISN'T YOURS

you used her and took
everything you could
you asked and asked
because you knew that she would
never say no
never turn down
never put you on blast
to everyone around
she'd let you take the light
away from her
but there is a painful lesson
that you must learn
it's that you cannot steal
what isn't yours
now you're shutting her out
and locking doors
let me know
why you're like this
always getting what you want
or you'll throw a fit
to those of us watching
it's clear to see
you don't know the definition
of family

BURNT

I burnt the bridge
just like you burnt me
and sat back and laughed
to me, it was funny
that you hurt me first
but I got the last laugh
I didn't have to experience it
your hurt or your wrath
I burnt the bridge
way before you could
I burnt the bridge
if I didn't, you would
I beat you to it
I won the game
and now, so you know
we will never be the same

TAKE AIM

you've got to step back
you've got to take aim
you can't let them think
that you've lost in their game

FALSE STORY

she knows who she is
she knows who she tries to be
she knows who you make her
in your twisted, false story

VICIOUS

children are innocent
children are precious
to rip them apart
means you're heartless
and vicious

WATER AND OIL

who cares if you're blood
blood can boil
one day, you'll realize
you're simply water and oil

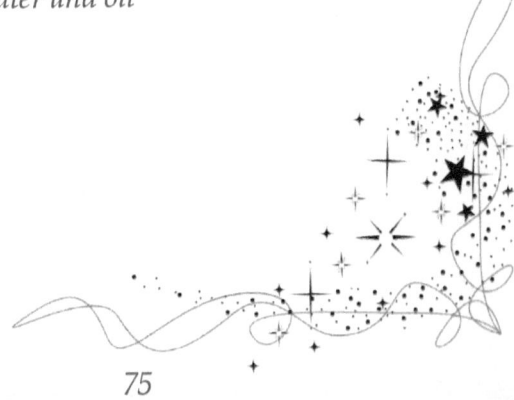

BROKEN INSIDE

Christmas is coming
everyone seems excited
around my family and I
you won't be invited
you're heartless and cold
the lowest of low
to pick on a child
is how far you will go
to show off your jealousy
to show your disdain
I'm sorry you felt it
but we won't feel the pain
you're broken inside
a soul, tainted with evil
it won't get to us
for we continue to live peaceful

FAKE

the only people who rip others apart
are the ones who didn't care from the start
it was all fake
they were never real
now, they can't help but express
how they truly feel

·•·꒜·o)·ọ·(o·꒜·•·

EXIT

the peace
the serenity
when the toxicity
exits your life
you can celebrate your successes
be happy for yourself
lord knows they aren't
happy for you

BLOOD

blood does not mean
they can steal your identity
your truth
what you've been through
they cannot rob you of
the progress you've achieved
you've grown through so much
for them to think less
proves they're so out of touch
don't let them dull your shine
keep yourself true to you
keep your priorities in line

SUCH A HATER

always such a hater
no one knows why
so many times
she's been close to goodbye
just once, it would be nice
to hear something good
a positive
a compliment
like a true friend would

NOTHING NEW

when you've always done something
and it's nothing new
you don't have to brag
about every little thing that you do

RISE ABOVE IT

constant ridicule
being put down
gets harder and harder
to smile
not frown
a positive attitude
she tries to keep
but so many nights
she lies in bed
and she weeps
no one would guess
and nobody knew
because all they're concerned with
is stunting her as she grew

OPPOSITE OF YOU

you look tired
well guess what
it turns out, I am
but the reason as to why
you wouldn't give a damn
I've been working and pushing
to make something more
I've never wanted something
like I want this before
sleepless nights
jotting notes
photos inside my head
I'm awake and still worrying
even as I'm in my bed
but I won't keep reiterating
saying what I've already said
you say I look tired
and that's because it's true
yes, I am so tired
because I'm opposite of you

MY FAULT

always watching my posts
but never a like
I really don't get it
there was never a fight
so why the constant attention
without a result
I guess I could delete you
then, that would be my fault

BEGGING

stay back
keep away
I'm begging you to
remove yourself
from my presence
like you usually do

NOW OR NEVER

the choice is now
the choice is never
you won't undermine me
you're not that clever
I know what I want
I know what I need
I won't change my decision
because of your greed
so when the choice is now
or the choice is never
I'll go with the first choice
always and forever

REMEMBER

you wouldn't be where you are
if I didn't leave
remember that when
your web, you weave

BORN AS A RAINBOW

she was born as a rainbow
but the colors, they've drained
and made her feel
she's absolutely insane
gas lighting and lying
it seems like the norm
as she grew older
she tried to reform
her thinking
her writing
and what she did best
she wanted to show them
that she withstood their test

CELEBRATE YOU

You should be celebrated
For victories large and small
Especially, when alone
You did it all
The only ones who do the opposite
Are the ones who are jealous of it
So be true to yourself
Celebrate your wins
Self-preservation is where your happiness begins

·•·ᘛ·o᙮.ọ.Co·ᘚ·•·

BACKSTABBERS

You'll always have haters
But what gets me is that
They'll talk about you like
At your table, they haven't sat

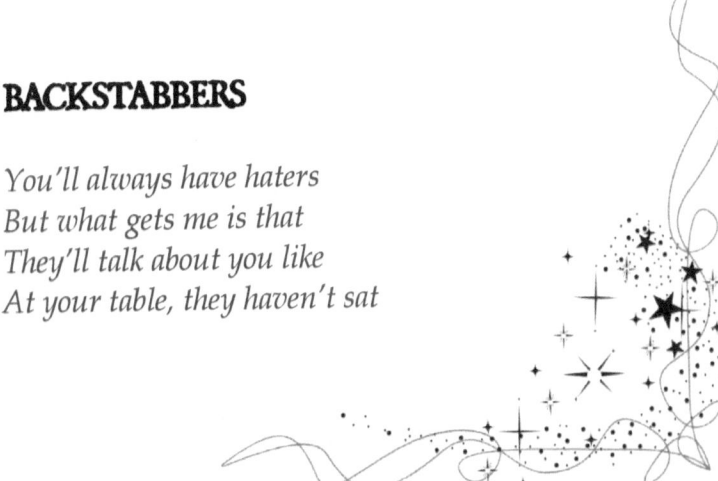

KNIFE OF PAIN

pain is so often caused
by the ones you love the most
the ones you hold close to your heart
because you would never hurt them
you expect the same in return
so, when the knife is pulled
pushed into your back
twisted and throbbing
it's that person you had
on a pedestal
those who meant the world
the ones you would have least expected
that's who it is
that's the cause of the true pain

JEALOUS CRITICS

She didn't want to believe
Hoped it wasn't true
That they were watching
Criticizing
Everything she would do
But it is true
And she was wrong
Now, she just wonders
For how long
How long were they jealous
How long did they hate
It truly doesn't even matter
Because to that, she can't relate
She's pure at heart
has a golden spirit
and she can sense toxicity
Anytime she is near it

ENVIOUS

where did it come from
when you threw me from the ledge
dropped me down
below the edge
what the hell caused it
you were fine in one moment
and the next, having a fit
I didn't see it coming
I wasn't prepared
I never suspected you
I figured you cared
was I wrong
yes, I was
now I'll write how I forgive you
just because
you need the love
it's so blindingly obvious
and I'll give it to you
just realize, you're envious

LITTLE GIRLS

little kids can be cruel
especially, little girls
they'll be cold and hateful
regardless of how it feels
to hurt a friend
to let them down
to make someone who always smiles
wear a frown
when your kids experience this
explain to them that cruel is a shoe
and the shoe fits
all those little girls
who are torturing them
and that she is the real one
she's the gem
the others are rocks
you couldn't polish them if you tried
after all, you did
but they continued to lie
lie and exclude
that's what they do best
but let your little one know
her head must rest

soon, she'll find friends who love her
they'll never take her for granted
she's a pure, loving soul
no matter the sour seeds they've planted

DEMENTED BRAIN

You've got a sick
And twisted
Demented brain
You bash and you bash
Constantly
For your own gain

WHAT SHE DOES

She is miserable
She hates her own life
So she has no issue
With stabbing you with a knife
Directly in the back
Or even in the chest
All she does is stab and bash
That's what she does best

RUSSELL

UNWANTED

you wanted it
I did not
you may have tried
but I haven't forgotten
what you wanted most
and tried to do
had it worked out your way
I would forever hate you
you would have ruined my life
even more than you did
thinking about it now
is like opening a lid
on a jar that sits, rotting inside
just like you are
you try to hide
the past and everything you did wrong
while I'm feeling guilty for letting it go on for so long
I'm so thankful that you didn't get what you wanted
my life would have be stalled
my growth forever stunted

WHY

where do I think this came from?
a world full of trauma and pain
why, is the question that is left
to remain
why that little girl?
why that time of her life?
why did you stab her with your poisoned knife?

· • ·≲·o)˙ö˙(o·≳· • ·

SHE HAD WINGS

she had wings before you clipped them
she flew higher than high
she had wings before you clipped them
you sick, perverted guy

FORCED STRENGTH

Her strength has been forced upon her
when she wanted to be weak
she couldn't or she'd be a goner

·•·⋜·o⟯.ȯ.⟮o·⋝·•·

THEY ALL KNOW

they all know who you are
you ran here to escape
but here isn't the place to play
for your truth, you're going to face

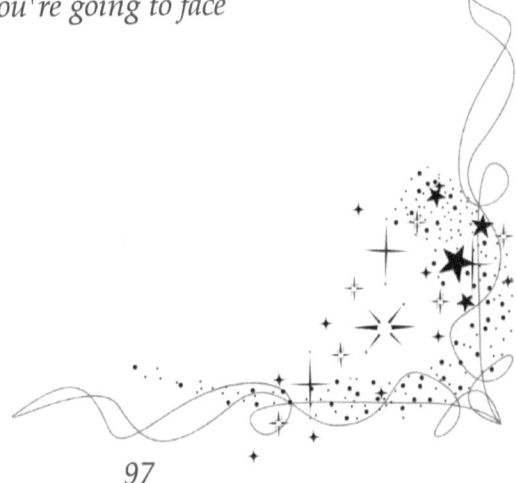

SINKING BOAT

if you know and you ignore
if you know and you cover
you're sick
you're twisted
the boat will sink soon enough

WRATH

it's okay to want vengeance
to release your wrath
especially when you
were forced down this path

VICTIM

often, people wonder how a criminal ended up
not often enough
do they wonder what happened to the victim
she has trust issues and problems
she can barely function
why?
because of someone they wonder about
because of him

·•·⋛·०⟩ְ₀̣⟨०·⋜·•·

VOODOO DOLL

I don't care if holding anger is like poisoning myself
I'd drink the whole bottle
and wish I were you
like a voodoo doll, I'd prick and poke
your entire existence is a damn joke

UPON A SLAB

I don't care if you feel better
I don't care if you're okay
I'm still holding out hope
of coming one day
upon a slab, I will stand and stare
looking down and asking
if you're burning down there

WILD SOUL

She releases her soul
Out, into the wild
Hoping it can reconnect
With that long, lost child
Help her repair
Hep her to grow
For he stunted her
More than anyone could know

THEY PLANTED FLOWERS

they planted flowers there
hoping it would erase the pain
but it doesn't work
it all still remains
they planted flowers there
hoping she would forget
but she doesn't
the past is what she regrets
they planted flowers there
he tried to change his life
but she won't let him forget
all of the constant strife
the trauma
the abuse
the physical toll
he made her out to be the fool
they planted flowers there
but now, how times have changed
she came back to mow them over
and to clear her name

SICK MAN

a sick man took her
he stole her pure heart
twisted her soul
into a piece of frameless art
who wants a tarnished toy
or mirror
who wants a child
who can't even think clear
he stole her pure heart
twisted her soul
and now that she's older
she's no longer the fool

TWENTY-TWO

if you were here now
you'd be twenty-two
and I'd be tied to a molester
forced to remember what they do

ENDING

The wind blew
The cold felt painful
On her beautiful face
She stepped into the road
Warm coffee in her hand
She knows she's about to
Find out how this
Will all end

YOUR FALL

while you may think you won
you've lost so much of it all
now, I'll sit back
and pray for your fall

PURE HEART

a sick man took her
he stole her pure heart
twisted her soul
into a piece of frameless art
who wants a tarnished toy
or mirror
who wants a child
who can't even think clear
he stole her pure heart
twisted her soul
and now that she's older
she's no longer the fool

YOUNG AND INNOCENT

I didn't like it
I know you think I did
I didn't like it
Why else would I have run and hid
So immature, so much to learn
so young and innocent
but I watched that burn
my childhood was lost
your sickness took from me
you sat back and liked it
wounds without making me bleed

CHILDHOOD BLUR

I don't have many childhood memories
it seems like a blur
so much was taken from me
but of this, I am sure
what happened to me
does not define me
it also does not and never could
confine me

GATES OF HELL

falling to her knees
she cried
in a second, it was over
she lost
where does she go from here?
what is next?
she didn't think she'd lose
she would have taken bets
he got away
he slithered through
to the gates of hell
she hopes he goes to
BLANK

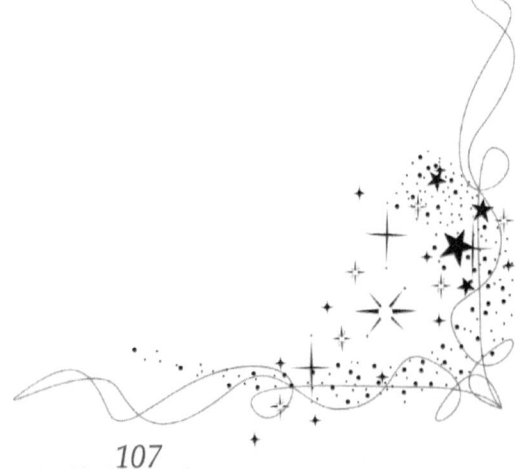

SNAKE IN THE DARK

SPILLING IN THE LIGHT

deep down, she knew
no shock
to the rest of us
a surprise
a secret
kept in the dark
but that's where you keep ugly things
in the black
seeping through the cracks
words, spilling in the light
no amount of sorry
will make what was done alright

SLIMY SPORT

cheating is such a slimy sport
not enough attention at home
and to trash, you'll resort

SHE IS

she is enough
she couldn't be more
but you pushed her aside
for some easy whore
don't say that it's because she's less
like you're something special
like you're the best

IN THE DARK

the next time you think you're the shit
remember, you were kept in the dark
where not a light was lit

HER HEART NEEDS A REST

he creeps
he sneaks and thinks she doesn't know
but she's got her intuition
she knows where it is he'll go
does she confront
or let go and let life take the wheel
she lies in bed and wonders
how is this even real
no one would expect it
or believe it's true
but he creeps and sneaks
he's even strayed too
to heal her heart
she must forgive
but how can one do that
and simply continue to live
it's hurting deep down and itching on her flesh
for now, she must forget it
her heart, it needs a rest

I CAN'T HELP HER

I know I can't help her
I can't make it better
but I can reinforce her strength
let her know she's endured more
more than this
more than the hurt she's wearing across her chest
the past wasn't long ago
but this pain
she needs to let go
release into the sky
into another realm
let the universe handle it
karma is real
but her feelings are valid
and she's certainly allowed to feel
hurt
let down
betrayed
it's all acceptable
what isn't
is letting herself think she wasn't enough

DEAR, ALCOHOL

THE ABYSS

drop the bottle down
into the abyss
you want to feel better
not keep feeling like this

ANOTHER DRINK

take another drink
you know you can't have just one
take another drink
without it, you're not fun
but that is your brain
it's tricking you
don't take another drink
to your sobriety, stay true

SOBRIETY

I don't mind if you drink
or if he does, or her
drinking is just not something
I personally prefer

POISIONING HER SOUL

she's got a week under her belt
it's the hundredth time
but she knew she had to do it
to drop the beer and the wine
it was ruining her body
poisoning her soul
and to do all of that willingly
is just so, very cruel

14 DAYS

Two weeks sounds shorter
than 14 days
but stand back, look
and count the ways
you've stayed the course
you've stuck to the plan
you took a deeper look
at what's in the can

TO BE SOBER

to be sober means
to feel all of the things
the happy, the heartache
the pain reality brings
but it's worth it, it's true
and soon, you will see
to be sober is what
is best for me

WHAT THEY'RE FOR

I've made it through some pretty stressful times
Sober
Now, I'm hoping that the stress is
Over
But if it isn't and there's some more
I'll lean on my friends
That's what they're for
They'll help talk me down
And tell me why I shouldn't
I'll be able to avoid a drink
When before
I couldn't

SELF BETRAYAL

more wine than blood
it's not okay
when you do this
it's yourself, you betray

· • · ⋛ · o) · ⦙ · (o · ⋚ · • ·

CHILLS

the utter chills it brings
to hear that could have been it
that could have been the last
it's a punch in the gut
a slap in the face
now is the time
but the past can't be erased

DEFEATED

defeated
I caved in
I lost it again
it was only a few days
since I had began
I need it to change
I need it to stick
because all of the back and forth
is making me sick

QUIT AND FIGHT

she lost herself in the bottle
couldn't see the light
but woke up and decided
it's time to quit and fight

·•·ξ·o)).ọ.((o·ξ·•·

FEEL

the days are longer
when you're not drowning yourself
you feel all the things
that you've forgotten you felt

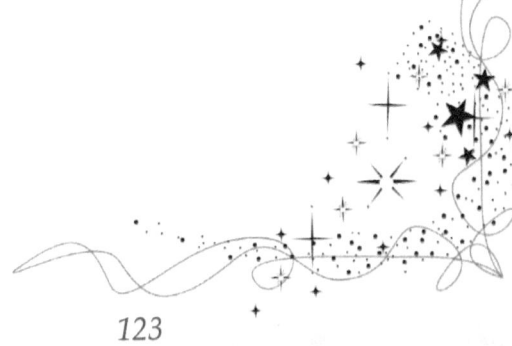

DEPARTURE

HURTFUL

It's hurtful to see
People you stood by
Walk away from you

BEST FRIEND, RUNNING

she ran from me
I never found out why
deserted me
made me feel like I could die
a best friend should stay
not leave you without care
be by your side
without asking them to be there

DISTANCE

the distance is making my heart burn and bleed

SHE'S LEAVING

walking away
she avoids goodbye
if she'd just turn around
you'd be able to see her cry
she didn't want that
she didn't want this
she's exhausted of the feelings
that you dismiss

GHOST OF YOU

memories with you are some of the best I have
but the ghost of you still haunts me

·•·⊰·o)·̥ʘ̣·(o·⊱·•·

NOT SURE I WOULD

if I could go back
walk the halls
rewrite the past
I'm not sure I would
the pain is too vast

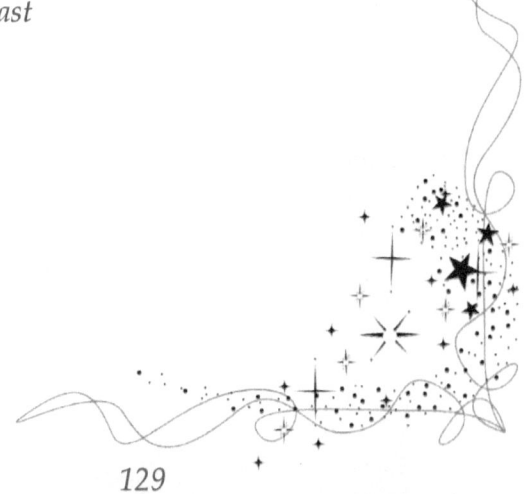

ABUSE

with every hit
you made me believe
I was nothing and it didn't
matter if I'd leave
with every degrade
her knife, inserted
twisting the blade
with every narcissistic attack
making me think
integrity is what I lack
the point of this is
you can get through it all
make it to the other side
if you just make the right call
believe it, there is always a rock
even if it is not
who you would have thought
go forth with this knowledge
and make me believe
that I know it does matter
what's the truth and what you see

SHE HAS A BOAT

she watched her drift away
the water gently swaying the boat
she had been the one
the only one
for so long
now that she has a boat
she's sailing away
she's no longer needed
it stings and it hurts
the feeling of nothing
but everything
at once
wanting to do it all
doing nothing
polar opposites
yet exactly identical
she's sailing away
and she can't stop her

END

Does she miss her
Or the thought of a friend
After all, she can't remember
What happened to make it end

·•·⧽·o)·ȯ·(o·⧼·•·

MOURNING

She's mourning a soul
That hasn't left the earth
She's putting her foot down
This time, she knows her worth

MISDIAGNOSIS

CLOUD

she's complex
at least, that's what they say
she's on cloud nine
bawling, the next day
showing a huge smile
making everyone around her laugh
feeling piles of bricks inside
hoping the feeling will soon pass
if complex is what they call it
then, that's what she is
she just knows deep down
she is better than this
better than how she feels
low, down
happy, not allowed
one day, hopefully soon
she will be back on that cloud

UNHEALTHY

your outside is perfect
inside, not so much
there are things in your brain
not even a therapist will touch
I'm unsure of what has happened to you
I tried and tried
but I just cannot get through
I was your friend as long as I could
you eventually left me
just like I knew you would

STRESS

it's normal to stress
it's normal to be
an overworked momma
with a touch of OCD
what isn't normal
is to let it consume
back to your happiness
you must resume

GRAVEYARD

she buried her emotions
so that the ghosts wouldn't use them
against her

137

HYPER

talking a mile a minute
can't sit still
fingers going on the keyboard
because writing gives me a thrill
I write of the good
I write of the bad
I write of the happy
I write of the sad
being hyper is a new feeling for me
getting everything done
feeling accomplished
feeling as if I have won
a prize in life
a metal if you will
being hyper is like torture
when you've got time to kill

NOT BROKEN, NOT WHOLE

I don't think I'm broken
but I don't think I'm whole
my soul has been tarnished
blurred by abandonment
pain and abuse
to go from one trauma to another
is tragic
a child who can't see the light
she grows into a woman
a strong woman, who will stand her ground
won't let others make her feel
she's less than
not important
that her feelings aren't valid
once a lonely little girl
now, a powerful adult
being not broken
is the end result

SOMEDAY

someday, she'll trust
someday, she'll thaw her frozen heart
someday, she'll be affectionate
someday, she'll be the one you miss
someday, she'll sit down and ponder
all of that
all of this
someday

IN THE GREY

when I'm in it
I'm in it
I'm so far down
I try to smile
but there's an internal frown
it's hard to be okay
this is how I feel
when I'm stuck in the grey

MISDIAGNOSIS

can anyone hear me?
does anyone care?
the word, misdiagnosis
as I sat in the chair
it is crazy to think
doctors could be wrong
but in this twisty game
I'm done playing along
tell me the truth
about who I am
don't write down a script
like it's nothing
and you don't give a damn
figure out the root of the cause
hearing misdiagnosis
is definite reason for pause
no wonder the medicine
that they gave me didn't work
this whole, entire thing
has me feeling berserk
but it's okay
I will get through it all
hearing misdiagnosis
won't cause me to fall

WHATS NEXT?

is there more?
of that, I am totally unsure
I don't know what comes
after this
but I do know that there is
so much that I don't want to miss
when I question myself
and ask what's next?
I look inward, to myself
and know that this answer reflects
the person I am
the person I've been
and to say there isn't more
would be a sin

TO SAY

To finally be able to say
I'm on the road to being fixed
Is something that no one without issues
Will ever understand

OBSESSIVE COMPULSIVE DISORDER

you've checked it already
but you'll check it again
did you check all the locks?
did you unplug the fan?
it's a tiring mental illness
something that drains
from its grip you wish you could escape
but you can't even explain
the reasons you check
the reasons you stress
all of this has
your brain in duress

DISORDER WARRIOR

her battle with the disorder
makes her whole life difficult
one day, she's being strict
the next, a free for all
she prays that into temptation
she will cease to fall
but so far
it is a battle
she loses
she comes out
on the other side
with battle scars and bruises

·•·ᶻ·o)·ȯ·(o·ᶻ·•·

HER DEMONS

her demons won't let her sleep
they scratch, they claw
they feast, they eat

144

BATTLEFIELD

sometimes, my brain feels like a battlefield
half is calm
the other, chaotic
it's a tiring place to be
inside my head
trying to explain it
proves even more exhausting
how can anyone help me
if I can't express the truth
these dark, twisted feelings
I get time to time
but it's not all the time
sometimes, it's flowers
the top of the shelf
it just depends on the day

CRYSTAL CLEAR STIGMA

it's a scary diagnosis
but only because of the stigma
people look down upon you
think you must be insane
you're not insane
neither am I
it's just a medical term
to describe our brains
they're a dark place to be
but also, very beautiful
one day, it's blurry
the next, crystal clear
don't let it scare you
I used to let it scare me
but it's just a diagnosis
it's not a definition of your soul

SOUL IS FALLING

when the darkness is calling
and you can feel it
your soul is falling
it is in, you must reel it
don't let it consume you
this very thing
you're meant to go through

GRAVE OF SADNESS

one day, you feel like you're on top of the world
the very next, you feel as if you're digging your own
grave of sadness

DROWNING

under water
falling further and further down
unable to see
water filling my lungs
screaming but no one can hear me
wishing I was above
back where I could speak
I'd let it be known
you didn't hurt me in the way you thought you did
you hardly even phased me
but I can't do that
because I'm drowning
so many things
rushing through my head
so many things left unsaid
will you remember me
will I forget you
who knows the truth
the only one right now
is that I'm drowning

DEPRESSION

a headache
you poor thing
a cold
get some rest
a toothache
that has to hurt
depressed and cannot function
shake it off
they claim it's just a spurt

PHASE

you're not always up
sometimes, it's a phase
you must sit back and realize
that everyone has rainy days

ACIDIC SADNESS

black swirls into total darkness
the ride has just begun
this is her life
her illness
it seems to never end
the adrenaline kicking in
sadness rains upon her like acid
she hurts
but she can't escape

HER

a soul without a meaning
a body without a home
a heart within a cage
a light without a bulb
a pen without the ink
a person full of rage
this, this is a description of her

MOODSWING

up high, energy off the chart
sudden crash, heavy weight on your heart
characterize, rule out
no clue what they're talking about
trying to find a way
to make it through the day
will anything ever help or cure
you'll never know
and I'm not sure

EMPTY & VOID

yes, I'm sad
no, you can't help me
it's something beyond discussing
it's deeper than the cuts
no one can help me
no one can light the candle
that I've blown out
time and time again
because of my insecurities
within myself
my being
all that I am
is empty and void

FROM THE BOTTOM

I'm trying so hard
to climb from the bottom
where I've found myself
yet again
it's dark and cold
down here
I don't belong here
I should be with you
I should be up and happy
I shouldn't feel this distress
I feel myself fading
will I make it out?
will I give up and rest here
forever

PRETENDING

mood up
mood down
wear a smile
hide a frown
rollercoaster emotions
wonder what the truth is
it isn't black
it isn't white
you shouldn't run
but you shouldn't fight
think in the darkness
turn on a light
for, come every morning
you have to pretend you're alright

BURNS IN HER CHEST

the stress is sometimes
overwhelming
it burns in her chest
her nerves and her patience
always put to the test
she knows that what she's doing is right
that doesn't stop the tears from coming
late at night
she's strong
resilient
doesn't take much of anything
but it's her own heart that she hears
feels it slowly breaking
the stress cannot define her
she has to release
she has to find something
that can help bring her peace

HAPPY TEARS

did you feel it
when you changed for the better
when you decided to turn it around
was there a sensation
were there tears
letting go of the pain
you've carried for years

JUGGLE

balance is possible
even when it's not
you can juggle tons more
than you would have ever thought

BLESSED

letting your wishes be heard
scary
not holding back a single word
question
is it going to work out
unknown
this is what life is all about
change
you hope and you pray
different
that you can move on but still stay
both
this is your deepest wish
hoping
you'll be blessed with this

ICE COLD HEART

ALONE

being surrounded by people
but feeling alone
can harden your heart
it can turn it to stone

ICE HEART

what is the cause
what makes it true
your heart should be red
but yours is blue
the color has changed
and that is because
you focus on being alone
hearing no applause
your heart is ice
that we know is true
but don't alienate yourself
that's the worst thing to do

LACKING HEART

The waves
crashing into the sand
her rings
reflecting the moonlight
off of her left hand
she wonders why she lacks heart
when she had it
back at the start
what changed
what made her fall away
she may never know
but forever, she will stay

SHOES

the path that she's walked
you couldn't even imagine
the hurt that she's felt
is more than you could fathom

COLD SEED

Her soul is as bright as the daytime sky
But her heart is still cold
And she thinks she knows why
Just a child, taken for granted
So young
And that's where this cold seed was planted

NICE

you do and do
for everyone you can
but their judgement upon you
it's in your hands
to decide whether you accept or deny
but it's clear to everyone else
their stories are lies
those who truly know you
know you're generous
with a heart of gold
but to yourself, it feels
as if it's turned blue and cold

HER MIND IN INK

LIKE A TIGER

The darkness within
Consumes every fiber
Of her being
But the light inside
Cannot be dimmed
For she knows her worth
And like a tiger
She will fight for it
To be shown

BAD LUCK

She's saturated in bad luck
But today brings good vibes
Every day has a little happy in it
For, it's how we live our lives

THE PATH

You are on the path
That's meant for you
That means there may be hard parts
You have to go through
But you have to stay strong
Keep playing your part
You know where you're supposed to be
In your heart

FORGIVNESS

being able to forgive does not mean you're weak
holding in resentment will only mute the happiness
you seek
forgetting may be impossible, forever in your brain
further down this road of life, you'll be proud of how
far you came
every experience, bad and good
have brought you to where you are
where you're meant to be
and surrounded by those you should

BROKEN

is this it?
is this the moment?
the end?
she's broken
so beautifully broken
the pieces shatter to the floor
what will she become
in this ending
this grand exit
who will she be
in the next life
the next lap around the sun
will all of her hurt and pain
be undone?

REALIZE

Take a breath
Close your eyes
You're already there
Take time and realize

.•.⸱⸲.o).ọ.⟨o.⸲.•.

ENDLESS SLUMBER

Her soul woke from an endless slumber
This is who she lost
She's coming back
Better than ever

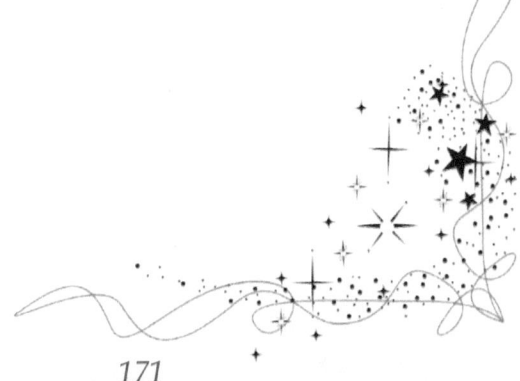

LIGHTHOUSE

standing on the edge of the cliff
in the dark blue water
stood a lighthouse
a place she could go to cry
a place she could release her feelings
a place she wished she never had to leave
here, she found peace
quiet
calm
the lighthouse was her safe place
for so very long

·•·‿·o)·o·(o·‿·•·

WEATHER

She accepted that people are just like the weather

FLY

The moon was bright
Shining in the sky
She let it all go
Allowed her stress to fly
Fly far and go away
With peace, she sat
And knew she'd be okay

FANTASY FACTORY

dreams are a happy place to be
unless it's a nightmare
when those occur
you wish you weren't there
inside your brain
in the dark mystery
you'd rather be in a dream
in the fantasy factory

173

EPIPHANY

it hit her like a ton of bricks
the thought of it
making her sick
she realized now that
her childhood was gone
and never coming back
life cannot be replayed
none of what happened to her is okay
but until this moment
she never saw the impact
the harm it had truly done
until this second
she never knew the true definition of
an epiphany

PRETEND

I won't act like I know
what you've gone through
every time I say that
I realize, I do
I won't pretend and I won't mislead
maybe to talk about it
is just what you need

THE GHOSTS

the ghost
and demons
of my past
haunt me until they have taken
every last
hope and dream
crushed them all
and left me with
no one to call

I WANT

I want to be better
I want to change
I don't know if that
can be arranged
I guess it can if I try hard enough
this year will be different
last year seemed rough
nothing crazy happened
nothing altered my soul
but I want to be better
I want my heart to be gold

FLOWERS GROW

flowers grow
where you plant the seed
a little love and water
is all they need
to sprout into beauty
for all to see
flowers grow
where you plant the seed

I WISH I COULD

I wish I could hold your hand
I wish I could walk beside you
I wish I could take some of your pain
I wish I could
I wish I could give you my breath
when you run out of yours
I wish I could let my heartbeat
inside your chest
when yours decides it needs a rest
I wish I could
I wish I could

TOUCH AND GO

we are so
touch and go
hot and cold
but all it would take
is an apology
an acknowledgement of
wrongdoing
hurt
lies
mental games
just say you're sorry
so we can be
fixed
healed
back to we

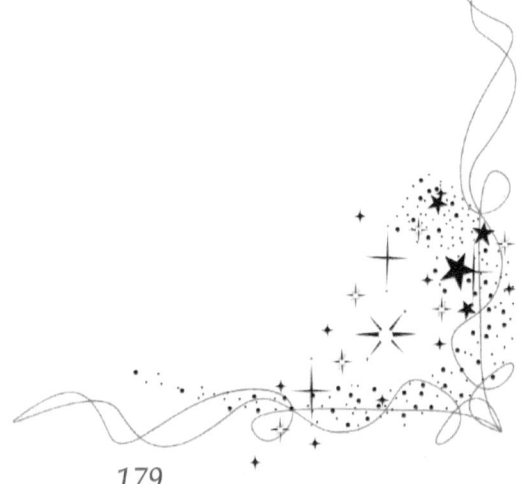

WHAT'S LEFT OF ME

when I'm torn apart
insides outside
what will be left?
what will they see?
will they see
what you meant to me
the scars and the damage
done by you
caused by years of games
the hurt too painful to ignore
there's got to be a better way
for them to discover you
the good times, hidden
need to come to light
am I the reason for your pain too?
your scars
is it me?
can you hear me?
when I call your name
what's left of the memories?
what's left of me?

MY APOLOGY

you never said sorry
so I guess I will
this distance between us
doesn't give me a thrill
I miss the good times
the memories
this can't be how
it's meant to be
this is it
my apology
I'm sorry for all that I've done wrong
I'm sorry it took so very long
for me to acknowledge
to accept my fate
I'm just hoping now
that it isn't too late
you're supposed to be here
supposed to be
in my life
around my family
don't you see
how special it would be
to have you

to have all of us
this is it
my apology

LOVING YOU

He went to bed
and didn't wake up the same
it seems that time
has brought a change
you want to alter it
but that cannot be arranged
this is the new norm
that he has to get used to
he can still love you
just like he's supposed to
I know it feels like you lost him
but he's still here
for that, you're lucky
he loves you too much
to leave you here
alone
stranded without him
so he held on
he stayed for you
he has a duty
to live up to
he's your father
the guide in your life

along this road
he's helped you more than you can see
and I am blessed to know him too
I hope he knows how much he means
to all of us
but mostly, you
he's loving you
like real fathers do

I'M PERMANENT

I'll stand here
I'll look you in the eyes
I'll tell you I'm sorry
that I apologize
but will you accept it?
will you shun me longer?
no matter what your choice
I'll always be here
I'm permanent
I'll never not show up
I'll never say no
you mean too much
you mean more
will you accept it?
or will you shut the door?

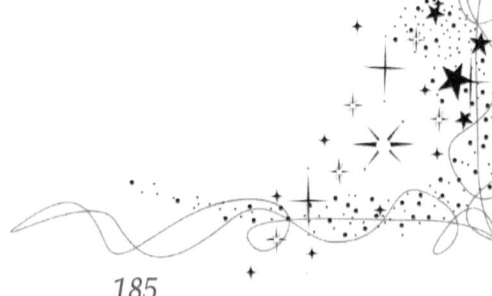

OUT OF SIGHT

the past is out of sight
so, it should be out of mind
it isn't because
she isn't that kind
the type to forget
the type to dismiss
there has to be more
more than this
the bad memories
and hurt
flooding her brain
she never knew she could
handle so much pain
but with the past out of sight
she's trying to get it out of mind
she's trying
she's trying
to leave it behind

MALIGNANT

it was a routine visit
how could I have known
that the skin tag they took
to biopsy had grown
and what was inside were cancerous cells
my instant reaction was pure hell
I had little babies
a husband at home
I couldn't be sick
it couldn't have grown
and spread within my body
of this, we were unsure
until a pet scan confirmed
that our prayers were
answered and that it didn't spread
but chaotic were our minds
until to that result, we were led

SINNER/SAINT

half of her is a sinner
the other half, a saint
be cautious that you
do not trust what she paints
the picture she'll draw
is her life
without flaws
but that isn't the truth
it is simply just lies
she'll be a damn sinner
until the day she dies

SOMETHING DIFFERENT

she knew from the start
this was something different
she knew in her heart
she knew in an instant

HOLLOW

I felt for my heartbeat
and felt nothing
so cold
so empty
what is in its place
nothing
there's nothing
it's just an empty space
it's hollow
it's void
it's been way too destroyed
so, when I feel for my heartbeat
there is nothing there
and I'm beginning to start
to not even care

DARKNESS

I want to walk into your darkness

IT'S OKAY, MOMMA

it's okay, momma
you're doing your best
you'll make it through all of this
it's just a test

MORNING COFFEE

there is just something about
that first cup of morning coffee
something about the quiet
the peace
that is early morning
but it wouldn't be whole without
the coffee

COVID

with a baby inside
I got the result
all I kept thinking
was that it was all my fault
did I not wear my mask
properly
is it going to hurt my unborn
baby
sleeping 20 plus hours
I sweated it out
couldn't take any medicine
so, there was another route
that had to be taken
with basically nothing
there was no one that could help me
despite my suffering
but I woke up one day
and it was gone
my son was born perfect
I think I knew all along
that he would
be okay
because momma stayed strong

every single day
even when I felt weak
I did not give up
I knew I couldn't make it
based on pure luck
to say that covid
kicked my ass
is an understatement
and I'm so glad that it passed

GOODBYE, 2023

saying goodbye to 2023
I wonder what's in store for me
Saying hello to 2024
I wonder what's behind this new door

·•·ᘔ·o)).ȯ.((o·ᘔ·•·

WHAT IF?

what if she lied?
what if she didn't?
about doing those things
that most see as forbidden
it's a true answer
that no one will ever know
she's trying to keep it close
but she also wants to let it go

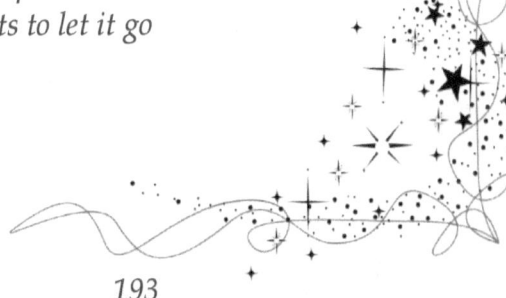

193

WHISKEY

I sat in the corner of a smokey
dimly lit bar
reflecting on all that brought me pain
this year and last
my findings were less than surprising
the things that brought me the most discomfort
are whiskey and you
one, I can go without
the other, I'll have to learn
because you are just you
but for whiskey, I yearn

·•·⪜·o).ọ.(o·⪝·•·

THREE LINES

I need you
no, I don't
yes, I do

BEAUTIFUL PAIN

to him,
her cry was beauty
her pain,
a symphony

·•·≾·o)).̣ọ.⊂(o·≿·•·

SHINE

just once
just one single time
let your heart believe
that people are kind
not everyone will hurt you
that is simply not true
just once
let their kindness
shine through

CHANGES

changes are what make life beautiful
when things stay the same
we are comfortable
but to be uncomfortable
usually always proves fruitful
a change is not a bad thing
it is a blessing in disguise

·•·⋜·o)·ọ·(o·⋟·•·

HOLIDAYS

The holidays aren't about who has the most gifts under the tree. It's about love, time and family

A WOMAN'S BODY

a woman's body is magic
the things it is capable of
a woman is truly something
that was sent here from above

·•·⛧·o⟩.ȯ.⟨o·⛧·•·

READING

reading is her escape
it unclogs her brain
it's her favorite, to sit
read and listen to the rain

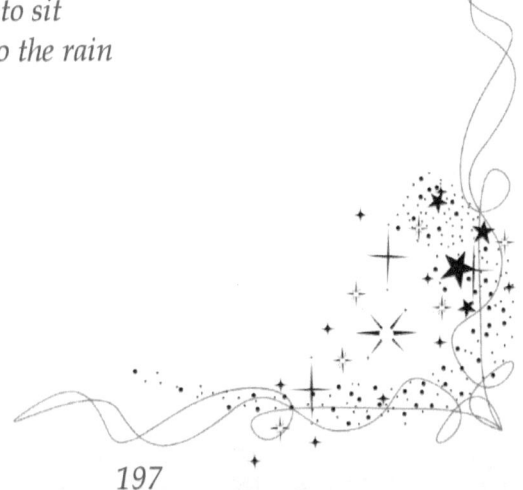

AT YOUR BEST

what a horrible feeling to feel
so broken and depressed
but you have little humans who need you
and need you at your best

·•·⋜·o⟩·ȯ·⟨o·⋝·•·

STUCK BETWEEN

is my soul really rotten?
or as sweet as a peach
both of those feel
they're way out of reach
stuck somewhere in between
I can't see the result
but I know deep inside
the answer is not my fault

STILL BLEEDING

a cut is made and years, decades later
it still bleeds
invisible bleeding
but the cut is still there
the tear in the skin
the gaping wound
it's all still there
you think, for a second, there's a glimmer of hope
that it's healed up
that it's closed
only to feel the stinging again
because you refuse to be
in a circle so mean and angry

SHE DIDN'T

the little girl thought she would fail but she didn't

BAD MAGIC

bad magic is inside her
just waiting to get out
bad magic is the one thing
she can't stop thinking about
she used to do only good
but now, she can't help it
bad magic is the magic
the only one that fits

YOU, MY DEAR

good things come to those who wait
isn't technically true
it comes to who works for it
pushes for it
and that, my dear is you

GROWTH

she is haunted by her past
why can't she let it go
she knows that leaving it behind
is the only way she'll grow

·•·⳽·o)).ọ.((o·⳽·•·

IT WILL GET BETTER

It will get better
It will be okay
It won't always be this way

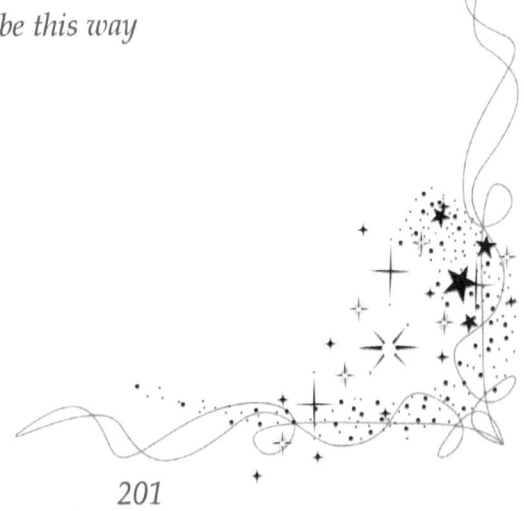

FIXING ME

when I look in the mirror
I am disgusted
how did I get here
how did I let go
to see me at my best
will my kids ever know
that I'm more than I look like
it's about what is inside
I try to mask my disgust
with that, I try to hide
I don't want my kids
to begin negative self-talk
I want to be strong for them
I want to be their rock
but when I see myself
I am truly let down
I must begin the journey
of fixing me
and showing my kids
the best I can be

CRYSTAL BALL

she looks up from her crystal ball
it's a damn shame to see how far you can fall
she sees all the truth
she sees all the flaws
I am sitting here, gripped
in her red, painted claws
she sees my mistakes
the roads that I took
with all of my mishaps
I could write a book
she can see all of that
but still, she does not judge
I want to hear the end
from my seat, I do not budge
is it a consequence of those mistakes
or a blessing from doing everything that it takes
to better myself
to crawl out of the hole
that I drug myself in
I've reshaped the mold
what does she see now
I dare to question
because I know this whole thing

has been a lesson
mistakes shape the future
mistakes built the past
she raises her hands
she ready to explain, at last

THE JOURNEY

it hasn't always been sunshine
it's been hard
it's been tough
I've felt at times
like I had taken enough
through everything though, I must say
it's been a beautiful journey
along the way
the journey and the road
are two different things
but with both of them
joy is what life brings
so while things may get hard
things may get tough
remember the journey
is beautiful enough

ROTTEN INSIDE

I had the worst luck
it seemed bad was upon bad
I couldn't make it stop
until enough was enough
I'm still left to question why
why did he do this
why did he do that
it's not my luck
it's his
and it's because he's rotten inside
it's his bad luck
not mine
I was just a piece in his twisted game

GET UP TEN

if you fall nine times
then, you get up ten
you may feel like it is
but it isn't the end
life throws us through loops
pushes us past the edge
but it's beautiful to look out
from the top, at the ledge
from that view, you see everything
you see all of the sites
if you get up ten times
everything is alright

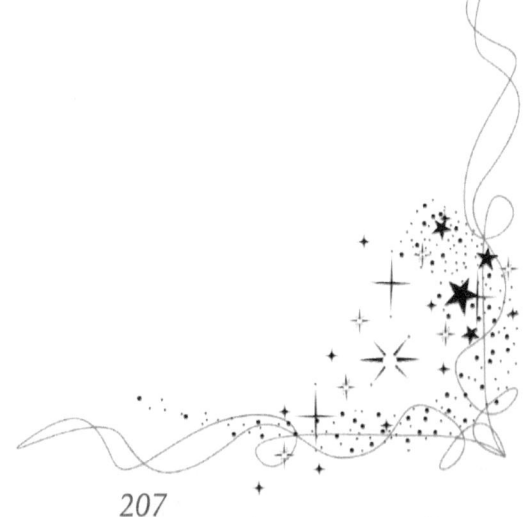

BEAUTY

I used to see blurry
like there was nothing below my feet
the nothingness took me down
further than I ever thought possible
fast forward to today
it's like time has healed my wounds
I'm awake
and I can see all of the beauty
the positivity that surrounds me
it's been there all along
it was just temporarily muted
so thankful I can see it now
it makes life worth living

THE GLUE

she is the glue
she is the one
she holds it all together
when it's falling apart
but who holds her together
when she's fraying
when she's coming undone
who comes to her rescue
the ghosts that dwell in her soul
they come to her aid
they sit with her
they comfort her
they lift her back up
so that she can continue
to be the glue

MAGICAL

learning the universe is magical
feeling the energy, spiritual
becoming who you've always been
like you've just discovered a long-lost twin
to crystals, you clutch
worship the moon so much
you love who you're becoming
the intentions overflowing and running

·•·⛧·o⟩.ȯ.⟨o·⛧·•·

ANGELS

the shells are like angels
pick them up one by one
remembering our loved ones
and all of the fun
we had during their time
here on this earth
and them knowing us
from the time of our birth

CHAOTIC CALMNESS

Even when she closes her eyes
The chaos creeps in
She tries not to let it
But the stress always wins
How can she change it
When she's trying to sleep
She'll never know the answer
It's a secret everyone must keep
From her
Not letting her know the way
So in this chaotic calmness
She'll forever stay

WISH AND DREAM

With a wish and a dream
She closed the door
She walked toward
What she knew she
Wanted more

FUNNY

isn't it funny how
we end up exactly where
we are meant to be
surrounded by the ones
we are supposed to be
life works in mysterious ways
even on the worst of days
because of those people
you know it's okay

FREEDOM

My soul
Wants freedom
More than my mind does
It is used to this
That and how it was

TAKE FLIGHT

I'm planning my first
Flight in the sky
I hope my nerves will be calm
And that I won't have anxiety
Or cry
With my brother by my side
I'll take that first flight
I think my mind already knows
It'll be fine
And I'll be alright

INSIDE THE WALLS

They can remodel the house
They can change everything
But inside the walls
Lives all of the things
All the memories
Good and bad
All of the fun times
And sad that they've had
It's all still there
And will forever be
But it's inside the walls
Somewhere they'll never see

REPETITIVE SLACK

I've fallen apart
And I don't know when
I'll ever feel like myself again
I miss the old me
The one who felt her best
Is this permanent or a test
Regardless, I have to get back
To who I am
And stop this repetitive slack

WHERE WILL YOU BE?

where will you be?
there?
here?
when the glass shatters
and you see the monster in the mirror

DROWNING

Her soul and her body
Are disconnected
She's swimming
Through emotions
She never knew
Even existed
That darkness comes
It swallows her whole
Fills her veins with spite
She can feel the pain
But somehow
Knows it will be alright
Keep swimming
Is what she keeps
Telling herself
As she drowns
She realizes
It's won
She's lost
She can swim
No more
She's not the same girl
That she was before

A Note From the Author

Glitter & Darkness was mentally taxing at times. Some of the subject matter brought me to tears, while others drew out rage and anger. My hope for this project is to help anyone going through similar situations and to let them know that there is a light at the end of the darkness. I refer to it as glitter. It's sprinkled everywhere and if you look hard enough, you can see it in the dark. Life is about who you surround yourself with. If they're the right people, they'll help pull you back up to the surface and they'll help you survive. Don't give up. It will get better.

A.M. Forney

About the Author

A. M. Forney lives in Pennsylvania with her husband, their three kids, Saint Bernard puppy and three cats.

When she isn't working or spending time with her family, she enjoys reading thrillers and dark romance, working out and writing.

Her first poetry collection, Forgiving Madness was released in November 2023. She has been featured in several anthologies and writes nearly every day, as it is her escape and something she truly enjoys doing.

Her work is posted on Instagram: @poetic_bookworm_ and Facebook: A. M. Forney.

www.ingramcontent.com/pod-product-compliance
Lightning Source LLC
Chambersburg PA
CBHW020232130626
46549CB00005B/1854